A Brief Introduction To Habits:

How To Create Good Habits and Break Bad Habits

Copyright © 2023 TYSON PHANANN

Visit our website for more inspiration, motivation, and self-improvement/ personal development info:

AchieveProgress.com

Table of Contents

Why I Wrote This Book

I wrote this book with a sincere intention of helping individuals navigate the maze of their own habits. I believe that understanding the power and structure of our daily routines is a pivotal step towards personal growth and self-improvement. Each of us is a complex bundle of habitual behaviors, some of which support our goals and aspirations, and others that seem to hold us back. It's this intricate web of behaviors that motivated me to write this book.

Over the years, I've observed a fundamental truth: many of us yearn to change, yet struggle to make those changes stick. It's easy to feel trapped in our patterns, uncertain of how to break free. That's why I set out to explore the mechanisms behind habit formation, to unearth practical strategies for breaking negative habits, and to offer guidance on how to build positive ones.

This book brings together the latest scientific research on habits, melded with practical strategies, real-life examples, and insightful exercises to help you transform your life. Whether you are dealing with cravings, combating stress, grappling with setbacks, or seeking motivation, this book provides tools and strategies to address these challenges head-on.

I believe that everyone has the capacity for change. By understanding our habits, we can harness this powerful force to enhance our well-being, achieve our goals, and ultimately lead more fulfilling lives. If you're ready to embark on this journey of self-discovery and transformation, I welcome you to dive into the pages of this book and start reshaping your world, one habit at a time.

With Deepest Gratitude,

Tyson Phanann

Why You Should Read This Book

You should read this book because habits form the invisible architecture of our lives. Whether it's the way you begin your day, the route you take to work, or how you unwind in the evenings, our habits powerfully shape our behavior, our health, and ultimately, our happiness.

This book is designed to provide you with an in-depth understanding of how habits work, why they are so hard to break, and the most effective strategies for changing them. With the knowledge and tools contained in this book, you will be equipped to replace detrimental habits with beneficial ones, helping you to lead a healthier and more productive life.

Importantly, this book goes beyond mere theory. It offers practical, scientifically-backed strategies that you can apply to your life immediately. From understanding the root cause of your habits to dealing with cravings, from using cognitive behavioral therapy to increasing mindfulness, this book will guide you through a comprehensive range of techniques.

Moreover, this book is designed to be accessible. It explains complex psychological principles in clear, understandable terms, making it suitable for anyone interested in understanding more about their behavior and how to change it.

In essence, this book is a guide to self-transformation. It empowers you to take control of your habits, and thereby take control of your life. If you're ready to embark on a journey of self-improvement, to understand yourself better, and to make lasting changes, this book is for you. It's more than just a book—it's a roadmap to a better, happier, and more fulfilling life.

With Deepest Gratitude,

Tyson Phanann

What Is A Habit?

A habit, at its core, is a routine or practice that is performed regularly, often unconsciously. It's a behavioral pattern that we embed into our lives due to repetition, forming an intrinsic part of our identity. Habits are integral to our lives, shaping our daily routines and our general approach to various tasks. They are born out of our brain's attempt to save effort, a function of its inherent ability to recognize patterns and create automatic responses to regular activities.

Not all habits are created equally. They can range from simple everyday actions, like brushing your teeth before bed, to more complex routines like the way you approach problem-solving at work. Crucially, habits can be both beneficial and detrimental. Good habits, such as regular exercise and healthy eating, can enhance our health and overall wellbeing. On the contrary, bad habits, such as smoking or excessive consumption of unhealthy foods, can harm our health and quality of life.

The formation of a habit involves a process known as the 'habit loop'. This comprises three components: the cue or trigger, the routine, and the reward. The cue or trigger is an event that initiates the habit. The routine is the behavior itself, and the reward is the benefit that reinforces the behavior. Understanding this cycle is key to creating good habits and breaking bad ones.

In the realm of psychology, there's a common notion that it takes about 21 days to form a new habit. However, more recent studies suggest it can take anywhere from 18 to 254 days, depending on the individual and the complexity of the habit. This reveals the highly personal nature of habit formation and the dedication it takes to ingrain a new routine into one's life.

While habits are often formed and executed unconsciously, becoming conscious of your habits can be a game-changer. Mindfulness, the practice of being present and fully engaged with whatever you're doing at the moment, can be a powerful tool in recognizing and altering your habits. It allows for self-reflection and the identification of habit triggers, providing an opportunity to change the routine that follows.

Habits are repeated behaviors that become automatic through a process of cue, routine, and reward. These practices have a profound influence on our lives and wellbeing. Understanding habits, their formation, and their influence is crucial for personal development and growth. It is through this understanding that we can harness the power of habits to transform our lives positively.

How Do I Create a New Habit?

Establishing a new habit requires more than mere willpower; it calls for understanding the mechanics of habit formation and tailoring a strategy that suits your unique circumstances. This process starts with setting a clear and achievable goal. Instead of setting vague objectives, aim for specific, actionable, and measurable goals. For instance, instead of resolving to "exercise more," decide to "jog for 30 minutes every morning."

Your new habit must be anchored to a consistent part of your routine, known as a habit trigger or cue. Habit triggers could be anything from time of day, location, or preceding activity. For example, your morning cup of coffee could serve as a cue to start your daily journaling habit. Utilizing existing habits to establish new ones can make the process more natural, a strategy known as habit stacking.

Commitment and repetition are crucial in the early stages of habit formation. When the new behavior is repeated consistently in the same context, the brain starts to automate the process, making the habit easier to perform over time. Some strategies to support this repetition include setting reminders, practicing visualization, or creating a routine that embeds the new habit.

Rewards play a pivotal role in habit formation. Positive reinforcement strengthens the habit loop, encouraging the repetition of the behavior. The reward could be anything that brings you joy or satisfaction, from enjoying a healthy smoothie after a workout to spending a few minutes in quiet reflection after journaling. Remember, the most compelling rewards are those that have a direct, meaningful connection to the habit you're trying to form.

Maintaining a new habit isn't always smooth sailing. You'll likely face obstacles and days when motivation runs low. Instead of aiming for perfection, adopt an approach of resilience. Embrace that setbacks are part of the process and that it's okay to miss a day or two. What's important is not to let temporary lapses turn into complete derailment of your habit formation journey.

Creating a new habit is a journey of self-improvement that involves clear goal setting, identifying triggers, consistency, rewarding your progress, and resilience in the face of setbacks. By understanding these elements, you can better navigate your path towards successful habit formation, contributing to a healthier, more productive, and fulfilling life.

What Are the Best Strategies to Form Good Habits?

The journey of creating good habits can be made significantly smoother with the help of certain strategies. One such strategy is habit stacking, a concept popularized by James Clear. Habit stacking involves integrating a new habit into your existing routine by associating it with an already established habit. For instance, if you're trying to cultivate a habit of meditation, you could pair it with your morning coffee ritual. This makes the new habit feel less disruptive and easier to remember.

Breaking down your goal into small, manageable tasks is another effective way to cultivate good habits. Known as "chunking," this strategy makes the new behavior less daunting and increases the likelihood of success. For instance, if your goal is to read more, start with reading a few pages each day, gradually increasing the number as the habit takes root. It's less about how much you do at once and more about consistency and repetition.

Visualization, the practice of creating a mental image or intention of what you want to achieve, can also assist in habit formation. When you visualize the process — not just the outcome — of your new habit, it can motivate you and make your goals appear more achievable. It's a tool often employed by athletes to enhance performance, but it can be equally beneficial for habit formation.

Moreover, maintaining an accountability system can bolster your commitment to your new habit. Sharing your goals with a friend, family member, or an online group can provide an external source of motivation. Furthermore, tracking your progress, either through an app or a traditional journal, can offer a tangible measure of your success and keep you motivated.

Crucially, focusing on the process rather than the outcome can make the journey towards habit formation more enjoyable and sustainable. It's about creating a new lifestyle and identity rather than achieving a singular goal. For instance, if your aim is to get fit, see yourself as someone who loves exercise, rather than someone who needs to lose weight. This shift in mindset can significantly bolster your commitment to your new habit.

Forming good habits isn't merely a product of willpower but of strategically planned actions and a well-structured approach. By utilizing strategies like habit stacking, chunking, visualization, accountability, and process orientation, you can facilitate the creation of habits that enhance your life and contribute to your personal growth.

How Long Does It Take to Form a New Habit?

The duration required to form a new habit varies greatly among individuals and is influenced by an array of factors. One commonly cited rule is the "21-day habit formation" principle, first proposed by plastic surgeon Dr. Maxwell Maltz in the 1960s, suggesting that it takes a minimum of 21 days to adjust to a new behavior. However, this rule has been widely criticized for oversimplifying the complexities of human behavior and habit formation.

Modern research offers a more nuanced perspective. A study conducted by health psychology researcher Phillippa Lally and her team at University College London found that, on average, it takes 66 days for a new behavior to become automatic, effectively becoming a habit. However, the study also found significant variation in how long habits took to form, ranging from 18 days to 254 days. The variation depends on the complexity of the habit, individual differences, and the context in which the habit is being formed.

Furthermore, it's crucial to note that the process of habit formation isn't a linear one. There may be periods of rapid progress followed by plateaus or even setbacks. Temporary lapses in practicing a new behavior do not mean the end of a budding habit, as long as the overall trend continues to move towards consistency. The key to successful habit formation lies in resilience and the ability to bounce back from these temporary lapses.

The concept of "neural plasticity" further supports the varying timeline of habit formation. Our brains continually change and adapt in response to our experiences. The process of forming a new habit involves creating new neural pathways and strengthening them over time, a process that can take varying lengths of time depending on the complexity of the habit and the individual's unique neurology.

While the question of how long it takes to form a new habit can be fascinating, it's equally, if not more, important to focus on the process of habit formation itself. Emphasizing the journey rather than a fixed endpoint can alleviate pressure, making habit formation more enjoyable and sustainable.

The time it takes to form a new habit varies significantly, influenced by a range of factors from the complexity of the habit to individual differences. Embracing this variability, acknowledging that setbacks are part of the process, and focusing on the journey can foster successful habit formation.

How Can I Make My Habits Stick?

Ensuring a habit "sticks" or becomes a durable part of your daily routine involves a combination of strategies, all deeply rooted in an understanding of your individual motivations, environment, and personal psychology. One approach to embedding habits in your life is through the "commitment device" strategy. Commitment devices are voluntary choices you make in the present that control your actions in the future, eliminating or reducing the option of falling back into old patterns. For instance, if you aim to jog every morning, keeping your jogging shoes next to your bed the night before can act as a commitment device.

Consistency is crucial for making habits stick. Our brains are wired to adopt patterns that are repeated over time, a process known as Hebbian learning, encapsulated by the phrase, "neurons that fire together, wire together." By repeating a new behavior consistently, the neural connections associated with the behavior are strengthened, eventually embedding the habit in our daily routine. Establishing a regular time and location for your habit can enhance this consistency.

Social influences can also contribute significantly to habit longevity. If your surrounding social environment supports your new habit, you're more likely to keep it up. Surrounding yourself with like-minded people who share similar habits or goals can offer both practical and emotional support, thereby enhancing habit persistence.

Making a habit enjoyable is another effective way to make it stick. In the words of James Clear, "the more enjoyable the behavior, the more it gets reinforced." The human brain releases dopamine, a neurotransmitter linked to pleasure and motivation, not only when we experience a rewarding activity, but also when we anticipate it. By finding ways to make the habit enjoyable or rewarding, you increase the likelihood of it becoming an integral part of your routine.

However, while it's essential to strive for consistency, it's equally crucial to have a flexible approach to your habit. Life is unpredictable, and strict rigidity can make your habit vulnerable to disruption. Building in some flexibility can make your habit more resilient to life's fluctuations and help prevent temporary disruptions from turning into complete cessation.

Making habits stick is a multidimensional process involving strategic planning, consistency, social support, enjoyment, and flexibility. By considering these aspects and tailoring your approach accordingly, you increase the chances of your new habits becoming a sustainable part of your life.

How Can I Make My Habits Automatic?

The transition of a behavior from a conscious action to an automatic habit is a fundamental aspect of human learning and behavior. It occurs when a behavior becomes ingrained due to its frequent repetition in a consistent context. Making a habit automatic involves a process known as 'chunking', where the brain converts a series of actions into an automatic routine.

One strategy to make habits automatic is the implementation of cues, which are signals triggering a particular behavior. Cues can take various forms, including a certain time of the day, a location, preceding events, emotional states, or other people. By consistently associating a behavior with a specific cue, you can increase the likelihood of the behavior becoming automatic. For instance, if you want to form a habit of meditating each morning, you could use waking up as a cue to trigger this habit.

Another crucial aspect of making habits automatic is repetition. The more a behavior is repeated, the more likely it is to become automatic. Regular repetition reinforces the neural pathways associated with the habit, facilitating its automaticity over time. Choosing a specific time and place for your habit can aid this repetition, as can attaching your new habit to an existing one—a strategy known as habit stacking.

Rewards also play an essential role in habit formation and automaticity. Our brains are wired to repeat behaviors that lead to positive outcomes. Therefore, incorporating immediate rewards into your habit-forming process can significantly enhance the chances of the habit becoming automatic. The reward could be intrinsic, such as the feeling of accomplishment after a workout, or extrinsic, like treating yourself to a favorite snack.

Maintaining a mindset of progress rather than perfection can also contribute to making habits automatic. Instead of focusing on being perfect from the outset, concentrate on small, consistent improvements. This approach, often referred to as the 'Kaizen method,' can reduce the resistance to new habit formation and enhance the chances of the habit becoming automatic.

Lastly, patience is a key element in the journey to making habits automatic. It's essential to recognize that the process of automating a habit doesn't happen overnight and will vary in duration depending on the complexity of the habit and individual differences. Holding this understanding can help maintain motivation during the habit formation process.

Making habits automatic involves a blend of strategic cues, consistent repetition, rewards, a growth mindset, and patience. By combining these factors, you can significantly enhance your ability to make your habits automatic, leading to sustainable behavioral change.

What Role Does Motivation Play in Forming Good Habits?

Motivation, an internal or external stimulus that incites a desire to act, plays a significant role in the formation of good habits. It fuels the initiation and persistence of new behaviors until they become ingrained in our routines. In essence, motivation acts as the spark that ignites the process of habit formation.

In the initial stages of forming a new habit, motivation is often high. It is during this phase that an individual sets new goals and begins to work toward them. This intrinsic motivation can be driven by personal interest or enjoyment in the task itself, or extrinsic motivation such as the desire for reward or recognition. For example, someone might be motivated to start a new fitness regimen because they enjoy physical activity (intrinsic motivation), or because they want to lose weight and improve their appearance (extrinsic motivation).

However, as time passes, maintaining this initial motivation can be challenging. This is where the concept of 'habituation' becomes important. Habituation is a decrease in response to a stimulus after repeated exposure. If the motivation for a habit comes solely from the novelty or excitement of a new goal, it may decrease over time, making the habit difficult to sustain. Therefore, it is crucial to find deeper, more enduring sources of motivation that can sustain a habit even after the novelty wears off.

One way to maintain motivation in habit formation is through setting meaningful and realistic goals. Goals that align with an individual's values and long-term aspirations can provide a more durable source of motivation. The process of setting and achieving these smaller, manageable goals can also provide a sense of achievement, which itself can boost motivation.

Progress tracking is another powerful tool in maintaining motivation. Seeing tangible evidence of progress can reinforce the value of the habit and provide positive feedback, which can increase motivation to continue. This can be especially effective when combined with rewards, offering an extra motivational boost when progress is made.

Another key factor in sustaining motivation is self-efficacy—the belief in one's ability to succeed in specific situations. Individuals who believe in their ability to execute the behaviors necessary to produce specific performance attainments are more likely to maintain their motivation over time. Building self-efficacy can be achieved through mastery experiences, vicarious experiences, verbal persuasion, and physiological and emotional states.

Motivation is integral to the formation of good habits. It kick-starts the process, sustains it through the challenges of change, and ultimately helps transform new behaviors into enduring habits. By understanding the role of motivation and employing strategies to maintain it, individuals can significantly enhance their ability to form and maintain good habits.

How Can I Keep Track of My Habits?

Keeping track of your habits is an essential component of both habit formation and habit breaking. It brings your behavior into focus and provides the information necessary for objective analysis and optimization. The act of monitoring can create a feedback loop that amplifies awareness, helps maintain motivation, and informs adjustments to improve the consistency and effectiveness of your habits.

Initially, habit tracking can be as simple as creating a checklist or marking off days on a calendar. For example, you might draw a box for each day of the week and check it off every time you perform your desired habit. This provides a visual representation of your progress, offering a clear indication of how regularly you're carrying out the habit. Over time, the desire to maintain a streak of checked boxes can motivate you to stick to your habit, even on days when your willpower might be lower.

Beyond the simple tracking, there are many digital tools available for more detailed habit tracking. Apps and online platforms can offer features that traditional methods cannot, such as reminders, analytics, and social aspects. For instance, habit tracking apps like Habitica, Streaks, or Done provide a user-friendly interface to track habits, set goals, and provide reminders. Many apps also include gamification features that can make habit tracking more engaging and rewarding.

Despite its utility, habit tracking needs to be approached with a mindful strategy. It's crucial to be realistic and not overwhelming oneself with tracking too many habits at once. It's generally more effective to start small, focusing on one or two key habits, before gradually adding more to your tracking regimen. This way, you'll avoid feeling overwhelmed and are more likely to stick with it.

Another important consideration is the duration for which you track your habit. While the sight of a growing streak can be highly motivating, missing a day and breaking the streak can be demoralizing. It's important to remember that occasional lapses are part of the process, and one or two missed days do not undermine the progress made on all the other days. Some people find it helpful to measure habit consistency over longer periods (e.g., a month or a quarter) rather than maintaining daily streaks.

Finally, remember that habit tracking is a tool to assist you, not a taskmaster. The ultimate goal is the habit itself, not the tracking. If the tracking becomes burdensome or a source of stress, it's okay to step back and reassess. You might find that a less rigorous tracking method is more sustainable and beneficial in the long run.

Habit tracking is an effective way to raise awareness, maintain motivation, and improve consistency. By selecting a method that fits your lifestyle, focusing on a few key habits, and approaching the process with flexibility and patience, you can greatly enhance your ability to form new habits and break old ones.

What Are Some Good Habits That Can Improve My Life?

A good habit is like a high-performing engine in a car. It continues to generate positive results even when you're not actively thinking about it. This concept lies at the heart of the self-improvement journey, where consciously cultivating good habits can lead to immense improvements in various aspects of life. Here are some notable habits to consider integrating into your daily routine.

To start, the habit of regular physical activity can have a transformative impact on both physical and mental health. The World Health Organization recommends 150 minutes of moderate-intensity or 75 minutes of vigorous-intensity physical activity per week. Regular exercise can help maintain a healthy weight, reduce the risk of chronic diseases, and improve mood and mental health.

Another powerful habit is mindful eating. Rather than eating while distracted or eating purely out of habit or boredom, mindful eating involves fully focusing on the experience of eating and drinking, both inside and outside the body. Paying attention to the colors, smells, textures, flavors, temperatures, and even the sounds of our food can be a more fulfilling way of eating and may help control overeating habits.

Cultivating a daily reading habit can also be enormously beneficial. Regular reading has been shown to increase empathy, improve memory and mental flexibility, and even delay cognitive decline. This doesn't necessarily mean reading dense novels or textbooks – even reading articles on interesting topics can be beneficial.

Maintaining regular sleep patterns is another habit that can dramatically improve life. Consistent sleep and wake times can aid in achieving quality sleep, which is vital for various aspects of health, including mental wellbeing, immune function, and longevity. Adults should aim for seven to nine hours of sleep per night, as per the National Sleep Foundation's recommendation.

The habit of practicing gratitude may not seem directly linked to tangible outcomes, but its impact can be profound. Regularly acknowledging and appreciating the good in your life can lead to increased positivity, improved mental health, and a more optimistic outlook. This could be as simple as keeping a gratitude journal and writing down three things you're grateful for each day.

Finally, cultivating the habit of lifelong learning can also significantly improve the quality of life. Continually seeking new knowledge and skills can lead to personal growth, increased confidence, and improved career prospects. This could involve taking online courses, learning a new language, or simply reading up on a new topic of interest each week.

Incorporating these habits into your daily routine can offer numerous benefits. However, it's essential to remember that everyone is unique, and what works for one person may not work for another. Therefore, it's crucial to explore different habits, be patient with yourself, and find what best suits your lifestyle and personal goals.

Can A Good Habit Replace A Bad One?

In the quest to improve ourselves, we often face the challenge of needing to replace bad habits with good ones. It's a common narrative: If you're prone to scrolling through social media late at night, swap it with reading a book. If you often skip breakfast, start preparing a healthy meal the night before. But does this approach really work? Can a good habit genuinely replace a bad one?

It turns out that it's not a simple substitution process, but a carefully navigated process of unlearning and relearning. The reason lies in the nature of habits themselves. When a behavior becomes a habit, it is encoded into the neural pathways of our brain. Each time we repeat the behavior, it strengthens the neural connection, making the action easier and almost automatic over time. When a habit is well-established, whether it's good or bad, it's there to stay.

However, this doesn't mean that we're stuck with our bad habits forever. It's more accurate to say that we can't merely erase a bad habit, but we can overshadow it with a new one. The process involves building new neural pathways and reinforcing them until they become stronger than the old ones. Essentially, we're teaching our brain to favor the new, beneficial habit over the old, harmful one.

Understanding the mechanics of habit formation and the role of our brain can be incredibly useful. For instance, being aware of the cues that trigger our bad habits is a critical first step. Once we recognize these cues, we can deliberately associate them with a new, desirable behavior. It's about creating a new response to the same trigger, thereby leading to a new routine.

Motivation and consistency are also key factors in this process. A good habit can only replace a bad one if it's performed consistently over time. It's also beneficial if the new habit has a positive outcome that is immediately apparent or rewarding in some way. This can help strengthen the new neural pathways more quickly and help us stick to the new habit.

However, it's important to manage expectations. The process of replacing bad habits doesn't happen overnight. It requires patience, time, and a lot of repetition. It can also involve some degree of trial and error, as different approaches work for different people. Therefore, understanding your own preferences and lifestyle is crucial when choosing the new habits you want to establish.

While good habits can't simply erase bad habits, they can certainly overshadow them. It's a journey of learning and unlearning, of patience and consistency, and of understanding our brains better. With determination and time, it's possible to reduce the influence of bad habits and let the good ones take the lead.

How Can I Be Consistent in My Habits?

Consistency is often hailed as the secret ingredient for turning actions into habits. It's the magical factor that bridges the gap between our intentions and our actions. But consistency, while simple in theory, can be a challenge to maintain. Fortunately, research and practical insights offer some valuable strategies for maintaining consistency in habits.

One essential aspect of achieving consistency is understanding the principle of gradual progression. The concept revolves around starting small and gradually scaling up. For instance, if the goal is to cultivate a daily reading habit, starting with a few pages or even a single paragraph can make the task feel less daunting and more manageable. This approach makes it easier to stick with the habit consistently, and as the habit becomes ingrained, it can be gradually expanded.

The principle of habit stacking, popularized by author James Clear, is another powerful tool for establishing consistency. Habit stacking involves coupling a new habit with an existing one, creating a strong link that makes it easier to remember and stick to the new habit. For example, if someone already has a habit of drinking coffee every morning, they could stack a new habit of meditating for five minutes immediately after preparing their coffee.

Creating a supportive environment can also make a significant difference in maintaining consistency. A well-designed environment reduces the effort needed to practice a habit, making it easier to stick to. If the aim is to promote a daily jogging habit, laying out running gear the night before can simplify the process and encourage consistency.

Setting clear intentions, or "implementation intentions," as psychologist Peter Gollwitzer calls them, can also aid in enhancing consistency. This approach involves formulating a plan specifying where, when, and how a habit will be practiced. Research has found that this strategy significantly improves the likelihood of following through on a habit.

Accountability is another potent tool that can be leveraged to promote consistency. Sharing your habit goals with a friend, family member, or a wider community can provide an additional motivation to remain consistent. There are numerous digital platforms and communities dedicated to habit formation that offer opportunities for such accountability partnerships.

Building consistency in habits is a multifaceted process that involves starting small, leveraging existing habits, manipulating our environment, setting clear intentions, and harnessing the power of accountability. While it's important to remember that every individual's journey is unique and there is no one-size-fits-all approach, these principles provide a solid foundation to start from.

How Does Habit Stacking Work?

Habit stacking, a term popularized by productivity expert James Clear in his book "Atomic Habits," is a powerful strategy used in habit formation. This approach involves integrating a new habit into an existing routine by associating it with a behavior that's already automatic, thus leveraging the strength of current habits to establish new ones.

The underlying mechanism of habit stacking can be explained by the Habit Loop model proposed by Charles Duhigg in his book "The Power of Habit." According to Duhigg, habits comprise three parts: a cue, a routine, and a reward. The cue triggers the routine, and the routine, once completed, leads to a reward. Over time, this loop becomes automatic, creating a habit. In the context of habit stacking, the completion of an existing habit serves as the cue for the new habit, effectively linking them together in the Habit Loop.

Let's illustrate this with a practical example. Suppose a person already has an ingrained habit of drinking a cup of coffee first thing in the morning. They wish to develop a new habit of journaling. By stacking these habits, the act of finishing the morning coffee would become the cue to start journaling. Over time, these actions can become interconnected, and the existing habit helps to root the new one.

When implementing habit stacking, it's important to ensure that the stacked habits are related or compatible in some way. For instance, pairing physical exercise with listening to a podcast can work well because both can be done simultaneously. However, trying to stack exercise with reading a book may be less effective due to the conflicting nature of these activities.

One of the reasons habit stacking is so effective is because it taps into the power of contextual cues, a concept widely supported in psychology. Our environments and the actions we associate with them can serve as potent triggers for behaviors. By using an established habit as a contextual cue for a new habit, the chances of successfully incorporating the new behavior are significantly increased.

Habit stacking works by associating a new habit with an existing one, using the existing habit as a trigger for the new one. It's an effective strategy because it leverages the power of existing routines and contextual cues, and it can be a powerful tool for anyone seeking to build new habits.

How Important is the Environment in Habit Formation?

The environment in which we live and work plays a pivotal role in habit formation. It is often overlooked but is a crucial factor influencing our behaviors. According to research, our surroundings can trigger both productive and unproductive habits, affecting our ability to establish and maintain new behaviors over time.

The theory behind the role of environment in habit formation revolves around the concept of cues. A cue is a trigger that initiates a habit. In terms of environment, a cue could be anything from the layout of a room to a particular smell. For instance, the smell of fresh coffee in the morning might trigger the habit of reading the newspaper. When we repeatedly act in response to these environmental cues, we reinforce the neural pathways associated with that habit, making it more automatic and less effortful.

Environments that are conducive to our desired habits make it easier for those habits to take root. For example, if you want to develop a habit of regular exercise, having a treadmill or yoga mat easily accessible at home can serve as a constant reminder and facilitate the habit formation process. On the contrary, an environment filled with distractions or barriers to the desired habit can hinder the process.

Similarly, altering the environment can be an effective strategy for breaking bad habits. By eliminating the cues that trigger undesired behaviors, we can disrupt the habit loop and make it easier to break free from detrimental routines. For example, if someone is trying to cut back on screen time, they might choose to keep their phone in a different room during work hours.

The environment's role extends beyond physical cues. The people in our lives, our social environment, can also significantly impact our habits. Research suggests that habits can be socially contagious—we tend to adopt behaviors that are prevalent in our social groups. Thus, surrounding ourselves with individuals who exhibit the behaviors we wish to adopt can help us form those habits more easily.

The environment is not just a background factor in habit formation—it's an active participant. It can trigger and reinforce habits, making them easier to form and harder to break. By being mindful of our surroundings and strategically shaping them, we can make our journey towards habit formation more achievable.

How Can I Use Triggers or Cues to Form Good Habits?

The principle of using triggers, or cues, to form good habits draws from the psychological concept known as 'the habit loop'. The habit loop is a neurobehavioral pattern that consists of three components: a cue or trigger, the routine or behavior, and the reward. By understanding and strategically applying this principle, we can successfully cultivate beneficial habits.

Cues or triggers are stimuli that initiate the habit loop. They can be external, such as a location, time of day, or presence of certain people, or internal, like a particular emotion or preceding action. The key to using cues to form good habits is to consciously attach a desired routine to a reliable, consistent cue. For instance, if you wish to cultivate a habit of reading, you could use the act of having your morning coffee as the cue. This way, each time you prepare your coffee, you are reminded to read a few pages of a book.

It's also beneficial to select cues that are naturally connected with the desired behavior. This takes advantage of the brain's associative learning processes, making the habit formation smoother and more effective. For instance, if you aim to jog regularly, use the sight of your running shoes as the cue. Placing your shoes next to your bed every night means waking up to them first thing in the morning, compelling you to head out for a jog.

Consistency is another essential aspect when working with cues and habit formation. The more consistently a behavior is performed in response to a specific cue, the more ingrained the habit becomes. This is due to the strengthening of neural pathways in the brain each time the habit loop is completed. Over time, the response to the cue becomes automatic, and the habit is formed.

However, the strength of the habit loop doesn't rest solely on the cue and routine. The reward—the positive outcome or feeling resulting from the behavior—is what reinforces the habit, encouraging its repetition. For instance, if the habit you're cultivating is regular exercise, the feeling of rejuvenation, accomplishment, or the visible improvement in fitness serves as the reward. This reinforces your desire to respond to the cue (your running shoes) and repeat the behavior (jogging).

Using triggers or cues effectively can expedite the process of habit formation. By understanding the concept of the habit loop and consciously implementing it in our daily routine, we can foster good habits more effortlessly and sustainably.

How Can Habits Improve My Productivity?

The concept of habits being able to enhance productivity stems from the psychological understanding that habits are automatic behaviors. When we form a habit, we lessen the cognitive load our brains need to perform that activity. As a result, we free up mental resources for other tasks, and this efficiency fuels productivity. When it comes to enhancing productivity, habits can be our most potent tool.

Productivity, at its core, is about making the most out of our time and resources. It's about accomplishing more with less effort. Good habits enable this by reducing decision fatigue. When actions become habitual, they require less conscious thought and decision-making, preserving our mental energy. For instance, if we establish a habit of sorting and responding to emails at a specific time each day, we no longer waste energy deciding when to do this task. It becomes a built-in part of our schedule.

Additionally, habits can help us break down big tasks into manageable parts, making them less daunting and easier to tackle. This concept, known as 'chunking,' is a well-established psychological principle. For example, creating a habit of writing just 500 words each morning can make the overwhelming task of writing a novel seem achievable. With time, these small chunks accumulate into substantial accomplishments.

Habits also help to create structure and routine in our day, which naturally bolsters productivity. With a well-established routine, our day has fewer uncertainties, less chaos, and more predictability. This order and stability lend themselves to a more productive and efficient use of time. For instance, a morning routine might involve exercise, a healthy breakfast, and planning the day. This habit sets a positive tone for the day, leaving us energized and ready to be productive.

Moreover, habits can also help us combat procrastination, a common enemy of productivity. We often procrastinate because a task feels too big, too difficult, or we don't know where to start. However, when we form habits related to that task, we reduce the barrier to entry. For example, a habit of studying for just twenty minutes a day may not seem like much, but it's a start and often, starting is the hardest part.

Habits serve as the cornerstone of productivity. By reducing decision fatigue, breaking down large tasks, adding structure to our day, and combating procrastination, habits can significantly enhance our productivity. Harnessing the power of habits might be the key to unlocking our full productivity potential.

How Do I Set Realistic Goals for My Habits?

When thinking about setting realistic goals for your habits, it's vital to remember that building new habits isn't an all-or-nothing process. It's about consistent effort over time, not immediate perfection. The first step is to set specific, measurable, attainable, relevant, and time-bound (SMART) goals. For instance, instead of deciding to "exercise more," a SMART goal would be to "walk for 30 minutes every day after dinner for the next month." This goal is clear, it's easy to determine whether you've met it, and it's reasonable.

Building on that, it's important to start small. Don't attempt to overhaul your entire life all at once. The smaller the habit, the easier it is to establish. Over time, these small changes can lead to big results. For instance, instead of trying to meditate for an hour each day, start with five minutes. Once this becomes an ingrained habit, you can gradually increase the duration. As James Clear, author of "Atomic Habits", says, "The most effective way to change your habits is to focus not on what you want to achieve, but on who you wish to become."

Another crucial factor is to align your habit goals with your broader life goals and values. If a habit goal doesn't tie in with what's truly important to you, it's unlikely you'll stick with it. For example, if you value family time, setting a goal to work for two hours every evening might be unrealistic. Instead, a goal to finish work by a certain time each day to have free time with family may be more effective.

Involving others in your habit goals can also be beneficial. Making your goals known to others can increase accountability, and you're more likely to follow through when someone else knows about your goal. Whether it's a coach, a mentor, a friend, or a family member, having someone to check in with can keep you on track.

Furthermore, be ready to adjust your goals as needed. Life is unpredictable, and what seemed realistic one month may not be realistic the next. Don't see these adjustments as failures, but as a necessary part of the process. Remember, building habits is about progress, not perfection.

Setting realistic habit goals involves making them SMART, starting small, aligning them with your values, involving others, and being flexible enough to adjust as needed. By keeping these points in mind, you can set yourself up for success in creating meaningful, long-lasting habits.

How Do I Break a Bad Habit?

Breaking a bad habit can feel like a monumental task, especially when it's deeply ingrained in our daily routines. It's not just about exerting willpower; it involves understanding the psychological mechanisms at play. One approach suggested by Charles Duhigg in his book "The Power of Habit" is to identify the habit's loop, which consists of a cue, a routine, and a reward. Recognizing these elements can help in understanding why a bad habit exists in the first place.

Firstly, the 'cue' is what triggers your habit. It might be a particular time of day, a location, a feeling, or even certain people. For example, the end of a workday might cue a habit of going to the bar for drinks. Once the cue is recognized, you can begin to address the habit. It's worth noting that avoiding the cue entirely can be an effective strategy, but it's not always practical or possible.

Next, the 'routine' is the habit itself, the action you automatically undertake in response to the cue. In our example, the routine is going to the bar and drinking. Awareness is key to disrupting the routine. By consciously acknowledging the action as it's occurring, you give yourself the opportunity to make a different choice.

The 'reward' is the positive reinforcement that follows the routine. It's what your brain is seeking when it urges you to follow the habit. In our example, the reward might be the relaxation and social connection experienced at the bar. Finding a healthier behavior that delivers a similar reward is a crucial part of breaking the habit loop.

A strategy for altering the habit loop is substitution. Once you've identified the cue and reward, you can insert a new, healthier routine. In our example, instead of going to the bar after work, you might choose to go to a yoga class, offering a different form of relaxation and social connection. This method allows the old habit loop to exist but changes its outcome.

It's important to remember that breaking bad habits isn't about perfection but persistence. Slips are a normal part of the process. What matters is not letting them derail your progress. Each time you choose the new routine over the old one, you're reinforcing the new habit loop and weakening the old one.

Engaging a support network can significantly aid in breaking bad habits. Friends, family, or a dedicated support group can provide encouragement, hold you accountable, and help you navigate setbacks. Breaking bad habits isn't easy, but with understanding, strategy, persistence, and support, it is entirely possible.

What are the Best Strategies to Break Bad Habits?

Changing a behavior pattern, especially one that's been embedded for years, can be a significant challenge. However, scientific research and practical experience have shown that certain strategies can significantly increase the success rate in breaking bad habits. These strategies include understanding the habit loop, creating friction, substitution, focusing on small changes, and seeking external support.

Understanding the habit loop - the cue, routine, reward cycle described by Charles Duhigg in his book, "The Power of Habit" - is essential. Recognizing the cue that triggers your habit, the routine you follow in response, and the reward you derive from it provides a framework for reshaping your behavior. By identifying these components, you can strategically manipulate the routine or reward to change the habit.

Increasing the friction or making the habit more difficult to accomplish can help break it. For example, if you're trying to reduce screen time, leaving your phone in another room can make it more challenging to mindlessly pick it up. Increasing friction works because habits, by nature, are actions our brains take to conserve effort. Making a habit more difficult counteracts this.

Substitution is another effective strategy, which involves replacing the bad habit with a good one. The idea is to identify the reward that you get from the bad habit and find a healthier habit that provides a similar reward. This strategy is based on the principle that it's easier for our brains to replace an action than to stop it altogether.

Focusing on small changes can also be beneficial when trying to break a bad habit. Instead of attempting a drastic transformation, aim for minor, manageable changes that will gradually lead to the desired outcome. This is linked to the concept of "Kaizen," a Japanese philosophy that emphasizes continuous improvement through small, incremental changes.

Finally, seeking external support can be an excellent asset in breaking bad habits. This support can come in various forms, such as professional counseling, joining a group with similar goals, or simply enlisting a friend or family member's help. Support networks can offer encouragement, provide accountability, and help navigate setbacks, making the journey easier.

Each of these strategies offers a different perspective and approach to habit change, and what works best may vary from person to person. However, by understanding and utilizing these strategies, anyone can increase their chances of breaking bad habits and creating healthier, more productive behaviors.

How Long Does it Take to Break a Habit?

When discussing habits, a common question that arises is the length of time required to break them. While it is generally accepted that habits can be difficult to change, a numerical figure that suits everyone is elusive due to the numerous factors at play. These factors include the nature of the habit, an individual's personality, environmental factors, and the strategies employed to break the habit.

To begin, the nature of the habit greatly influences how long it may take to break it. For example, a minor habit such as biting nails might take less time to overcome compared to a deep-seated smoking addiction. This is because the more ingrained a habit is in our routine, the harder it is to break. The habit's complexity, intensity, and the extent of its integration into our daily lives play significant roles.

Individual personality and characteristics are also crucial considerations. People with high levels of self-discipline, motivation, and a strong understanding of their triggers and cues might find it easier to break habits compared to others. Personal beliefs and attitudes towards the habit and the change process also matter. A person who is highly motivated to quit a habit for health or personal reasons will likely find it easier than someone who is ambivalent about making the change.

Environment plays an essential role too. A supportive and conducive environment can expedite the habit-breaking process. This can include living or working in environments that reduce exposure to triggers of the habit or being surrounded by supportive individuals who are aware and respectful of your goals.

Lastly, the strategy adopted to break the habit is a deciding factor. Approaches that incorporate the principles of behavior change, such as habit substitution, trigger elimination, and gradual changes, tend to be more effective. Hence, using such scientifically backed strategies might help quicken the habit-breaking process.

An often-quoted figure is "21 days to break a habit," derived from observations made by plastic surgeon Dr. Maxwell Maltz in the 1960s. However, recent research, such as a study led by Phillippa Lally at University College London, suggests that it takes 66 days on average for a habit to become automatic or for an old habit to be broken. Yet, it's important to remember this is an average, and the time can vary greatly between individuals and habits.

The time it takes to break a habit is not set in stone and is influenced by various personal and environmental factors. It's crucial to remember that habit change is a personal journey, and progress may not always be linear. Setbacks can happen, and patience with oneself during the process is key.

How Can I Replace a Bad Habit with a Good One?

Initiating the process of replacing a bad habit with a good one requires a nuanced understanding of the intricate mechanisms that power our habits. Habits, in essence, are composed of three main parts: a cue or trigger, the routine or behavior, and the reward. This structure is often referred to as the habit loop, a term popularized by Charles Duhigg in his book 'The Power of Habit'. Understanding and manipulating this loop can significantly aid in the endeavor of habit replacement.

Recognizing the cue or trigger is the first step towards replacing a bad habit. A cue is an event or situation that triggers the habit. It could be a time of the day, an emotion, a place, or the presence of particular people or circumstances. Being conscious and mindful about the triggers of our unwanted habits can provide insight into why and when we engage in certain behaviors. For example, do you find yourself reaching for unhealthy snacks when you are stressed? In this case, stress would be the trigger.

Once the cue has been identified, the next step is to determine the routine, which is the behavior you want to change. It's important to look at the behavior without judgement, simply as a response to the identified trigger. Continuing with the previous example, the routine is the act of reaching for unhealthy snacks. At this point, it's essential to clarify what the new, desired behavior is. Perhaps instead of reaching for unhealthy snacks, you would like to reach for a piece of fruit, go for a quick walk, or practice a few minutes of deep breathing to manage your stress.

The final component of the habit loop is the reward. Rewards are the benefits or positive feelings that the habit gives us and the reason why we keep repeating the behavior. It's important to choose a new habit that delivers a similar reward to the old one. For instance, if eating snacks was a way to cope with stress, the new habit should also help manage stress. That's why it's crucial to choose a replacement habit that is enjoyable and satisfying, as it increases the likelihood of the new habit sticking.

Following these steps and consciously repeating the new behavior in response to the trigger will over time lead to the formation of a new habit loop. This process might take time and patience, but it is certainly achievable. It is also worth noting that it is often easier and more effective to replace a bad habit than to completely eliminate it without substitution.

Habit change isn't a one-size-fits-all solution. It's a personal journey that requires introspection, self-compassion, and resilience. Setbacks may occur, but each attempt brings you closer to making the change permanent. With consistency and commitment, replacing a bad habit with a good one can become a reality.

How Can I Deal with the Cravings that Come When Trying to Break a Habit?

Cravings are a natural part of the process when attempting to break a habit. These strong desires can be seen as a physiological and psychological response to the absence of a behavior that our body or mind has grown accustomed to. Whether it's craving for a cigarette when trying to quit smoking or the temptation to eat sweets while following a healthier diet, these cravings can be powerful and sometimes overwhelming. However, with a strategic approach and understanding, it is entirely possible to manage these cravings and successfully break the habit.

The first approach to deal with cravings is to understand their true nature. Cravings are often not about the object of desire itself, but rather the emotional state it provides. As an example, someone might crave a cigarette not because they enjoy the taste of smoke, but because smoking provides a temporary relief from stress or anxiety. Recognizing this fact can help one to replace the craving with a healthier behavior that brings about the same emotional state, like deep breathing or meditating when feeling stressed.

Cravings are also linked to specific triggers, which are often tied to certain situations, times, or emotions. Identifying these triggers can be a powerful tool in managing cravings. If a certain time of the day or a specific situation consistently sparks a craving, being aware of this pattern can prepare you mentally to counter it. Changing routines or environments that are associated with the craving can also be beneficial. For instance, if you typically have a cigarette with your morning coffee, you could try switching to tea or taking a short walk instead.

Another strategy is to delay the response to a craving. Instead of immediately giving in, try to wait for a few minutes. During this time, engage in a distracting activity. Often, the intensity of the craving will decrease over time. It's important to remember that cravings are transient and will eventually pass, even if they aren't satisfied.

Mindfulness is a useful tool in managing cravings. It involves staying present and fully experiencing the craving rather than trying to ignore it or push it away. Studies have shown that practicing mindfulness can help reduce the intensity of cravings. This approach involves noticing the thoughts, feelings, and physical sensations that come with the craving without judging or acting on them.

Lastly, maintaining a supportive environment can make a significant difference. Surrounding yourself with people who understand and support your goal can provide the extra motivation needed to resist cravings. Support can come from friends, family, or support groups of people who are facing similar challenges.

While cravings are an inevitable part of breaking a habit, they don't have to dictate the process. Understanding, patience, and strategic planning can help manage cravings, making the journey towards breaking a habit more manageable and eventually, successful.

Can I Completely Eliminate a Habit, or Does it Just Get Replaced?

The power of habits in shaping our everyday lives is well-established. Once entrenched, they act as automatic responses, enabling us to perform complex tasks with little conscious thought. But what happens when we aim to eliminate a habit? Is it possible to entirely eradicate a habit, or do we simply replace it with a new one?

The concept of habit elimination is indeed quite complex. Habits, particularly those deeply ingrained, are hard to remove completely because they reside within our neural pathways. According to the renowned neurologist, Donald Hebb, "neurons that fire together, wire together." What this implies is that the repetitive nature of habits strengthens the neural connections, embedding them deeper into our brain's architecture. Therefore, the habit remains within the network, ready to be triggered, even if we stop performing it.

However, this doesn't mean change is impossible. As challenging as it might be, the human brain is remarkably adaptable, a quality scientists refer to as neuroplasticity. Neuroplasticity allows us to form new neural connections throughout life as we acquire new knowledge or skills. This adaptability of the brain forms the basis of habit replacement, a strategy widely recognized as being more effective than trying to eliminate a habit outright.

Habit replacement operates on the principle of changing the routine part of the habit loop while keeping the cue and the reward intact. This approach was popularized by Charles Duhigg in his book "The Power of Habit." For instance, if someone has a habit of eating cookies when they feel stressed (cue: stress, routine: eating cookies, reward: stress relief), they could replace the routine of eating cookies with taking a short walk or practicing deep breathing exercises. The new activity should ideally offer a similar reward, in this case, relief from stress.

So, while it might be difficult to completely eliminate a habit, it is feasible and often more effective to replace it with a more desirable one. Recognizing the cues and rewards associated with the habit is the first step in this process. The next is selecting an alternative routine that delivers a similar reward. With time and consistent practice, the new habit can replace the old one, reshaping the neural connections and leading to healthier behavior patterns.

It's crucial to remember that change doesn't happen overnight. Both patience and persistence are needed in this journey of transformation. It's also helpful to understand that setbacks are part of the process, not an indication of failure. With each step, even small ones, you're retraining your brain, replacing an old, undesired habit with a new, more beneficial one.

How Can I Keep Myself Motivated While Trying to Break a Bad Habit?

Breaking a bad habit can be a challenging endeavor. The process demands consistent effort, persistence, and an unflinching dedication to change. Yet, one of the most vital elements in this journey is maintaining motivation. But how does one keep the fires of motivation burning when the road to change is paved with obstacles?

To answer this question, we must first understand that motivation is not a constant state. It ebbs and flows, influenced by various factors like our mood, energy levels, and even the immediate environment. This knowledge empowers us to design strategies that can help maintain or reignite motivation, even when it wanes.

A cornerstone of motivation in the context of habit change is setting clear, achievable goals. Instead of aiming to completely eliminate the habit immediately, focus on progressive reduction. For instance, if the habit is smoking, start by reducing the number of cigarettes per day. Celebrating these small victories along the journey can provide a significant motivational boost, creating a positive feedback loop that makes the process less daunting.

Visualization is another potent tool for staying motivated. By creating a mental image of the desired outcome, you can reinforce the reasons why you embarked on the habit change journey. Remember, the more vivid and detailed the visualization, the more compelling it will be.

Another factor crucial to sustaining motivation is self-compassion. Breaking a bad habit often involves setbacks. Instead of viewing these as failures, treat them as learning opportunities. Show yourself the same kindness and understanding you would extend to a friend in a similar situation. Self-compassion fosters resilience, allowing you to bounce back from setbacks more readily and keep your motivation intact.

Staying connected with a supportive community or seeking the help of a coach or mentor can also provide an essential motivational lift. The social aspect of this strategy can help counter feelings of isolation and provide encouragement when challenges seem insurmountable. Knowing that others believe in your ability to change can be a significant motivator.

Finally, mindfulness practices like meditation can be incredibly beneficial in maintaining motivation. By increasing your awareness of your thoughts and feelings, these practices can help you identify negative patterns that can sap your motivation and address them effectively.

Keeping motivation alive while trying to break a bad habit involves a combination of clear goal-setting, visualization, self-compassion, seeking social support, and mindfulness practices. Remember, the journey towards breaking a bad habit is often not a straight path but a winding road with ups and downs. Recognizing this and employing strategies to sustain motivation can make the journey more manageable and ultimately lead to successful habit change.

What Role Does Willpower Play in Breaking Bad Habits?

Understanding the role of willpower in the journey of breaking bad habits can be essential to successfully replace those habits with healthier ones. Willpower, also known as self-control, is the ability to resist short-term temptations or distractions in order to achieve long-term goals. It's like a muscle that can be strengthened with practice and can play a significant part in our capacity to overcome undesirable habits.

In the context of habits, it's important to note that every habit consists of a cue, a routine, and a reward. The role of willpower becomes critical in overriding the routine part of this loop. For instance, if an individual is trying to quit smoking, the cue might be a stressful situation, the routine is the act of smoking, and the reward could be the temporary relief it provides. In this scenario, exercising willpower can help the individual resist the urge to smoke when they encounter the cue.

However, relying solely on willpower might not be the most effective strategy for long-term habit change. While willpower can get you started, maintaining a change in behavior over time typically requires more than just mental strength. The key lies in leveraging your willpower to create new, healthier routines that can eventually become automatic, thus less reliant on constant conscious effort.

A more sustainable approach can be focusing on structuring your environment in a way that supports your new habits and reduces the need for willpower. By altering the cues or making the undesirable routine more difficult to engage in, you can make it easier to break the habit. For example, if you're trying to quit eating junk food, you could avoid keeping it at home. This environmental change reduces the need for willpower as the cue (seeing junk food) is removed.

Willpower is also believed to be a limited resource that gets depleted as you use it. This phenomenon, known as ego depletion, suggests that if you've been resisting temptations all day, your willpower 'muscle' might be tired and less effective by the end of the day. Understanding this can help you plan your day and tasks in a way that requires less willpower later when it's likely to be low.

Lastly, studies suggest that our beliefs about willpower can influence how it works for us. If you believe that your willpower is a limited resource, you're likely to feel depleted after a challenging task. But if you believe that willpower is self-renewing, you're likely to have a higher capacity for self-control, even when faced with repeated challenges.

While willpower plays a crucial role in breaking bad habits, its power lies not in constant application but rather in strategic utilization. By using your willpower to design a conducive environment and establish new, healthier routines, you can maximize its benefits. Balancing willpower with other strategies can make the journey to breaking bad habits more sustainable and successful.

How Does Stress Affect Bad Habits?

Stress has a profound impact on our habits, especially those considered undesirable. As humans, we're naturally inclined to seek comfort in response to stressful situations, and often, this manifests as the resurgence of bad habits or the formation of new ones. Under stress, our brains crave familiar patterns and routines, including those that aren't beneficial in the long run. Whether it's overeating, smoking, or procrastinating, the adverse actions serve as a form of immediate stress relief, even if the relief is temporary.

The link between stress and bad habits can be traced back to the brain's reward system. Stress triggers the release of a hormone known as cortisol, which can lead to increased cravings for rewards. When the 'reward' comes in the form of a bad habit, such as junk food or cigarettes, this can reinforce the habit loop, making it even harder to break free. Stress can also impair our ability to exercise self-control, further fueling the cycle of bad habits.

Interestingly, the relationship between stress and bad habits is bidirectional. Just as stress can lead to bad habits, these habits can also increase stress levels, creating a vicious cycle. For instance, someone who resorts to excessive alcohol consumption as a stress-coping mechanism might experience increased stress due to health problems or relationship issues caused by their drinking habit.

To mitigate the effect of stress on bad habits, one effective approach is to develop healthy stress-management techniques. These could include mindfulness meditation, regular exercise, or talking things out with friends or a professional counselor. By managing stress effectively, the temptation to resort to bad habits can be significantly reduced.

Another effective strategy is to understand and modify the habit loop of cues, routines, and rewards. If stress is a cue that triggers a bad habit, finding a different, healthier routine can help break this loop. For example, if someone tends to eat junk food when stressed, they could replace this routine with a healthier one, like going for a walk or practicing deep-breathing exercises.

Stress can indeed exacerbate bad habits, understanding this relationship can equip us with strategies to mitigate its effects. Through effective stress management and conscious habit modification, it's possible to break the cycle and replace bad habits with healthier ones. Awareness of how our brains react to stress is the first step towards this goal.

How Can I Avoid Falling Back Into Old Habits?

Avoiding the relapse into old habits, particularly those that are detrimental, requires understanding, strategy, and consistent effort. The first step is gaining insight into the habit loop, which consists of a cue, routine, and reward. Understanding this loop allows for strategic intervention at various points, helping to curb the habit's recurrence. Recognizing the cues that trigger the habit, altering the routine, or modifying the reward are all effective ways to disrupt the cycle.

It's also important to replace old habits with new ones rather than trying to eliminate a habit altogether. Habits are hardwired into our neural pathways, making them extremely resistant to eradication. By substituting a bad habit with a healthier alternative, the same neural pathway can be utilized, but in a more beneficial way. For example, if you habitually snack on junk food when you're bored, you could replace this routine with drinking water or eating a piece of fruit.

Maintaining consistency is vital in avoiding a fallback into old habits. Habits are established through repetition, and the same principle applies when trying to change them. The more often you engage in the new behavior, the stronger the neural connections become, increasing the likelihood of the new habit sticking. It's also crucial to be patient, as changing habits is a slow process that may involve occasional setbacks.

Building a supportive environment can significantly aid in habit change. This could involve eliminating triggers in your surroundings or getting friends and family to support your efforts. For instance, if you're trying to quit smoking, getting rid of all cigarettes and lighters around you and seeking support from loved ones or a support group can be immensely helpful.

Having a contingency plan for dealing with setbacks can also prevent you from falling back into old habits. Rather than viewing a lapse as a failure, see it as an opportunity for learning and adjusting your strategies. Resilience and a positive mindset play a crucial role in successful habit change.

Self-awareness and mindfulness can help you catch yourself before falling back into old habits. Paying attention to your thoughts, feelings, and behaviors can allow you to notice when you're veering off course and make the necessary corrections. Regular practices like meditation can enhance your mindfulness skills and help you stay focused on your goal.

How Does Understanding the Root Cause of a Habit Help in Breaking It?

Breaking a habit often goes beyond mere willpower and discipline; it requires a deeper understanding of the habit itself, particularly its root cause. The roots of habits lie in the associations our brains have made between a situation, a behavior, and a reward. This understanding can be enlightening, as it provides a glimpse into the ways we have trained ourselves, often unconsciously, to behave in certain ways in response to specific cues.

Knowing the root cause of a habit allows us to examine it critically. Once we understand why a habit exists and the function it serves, we can begin to address the issue more effectively. For instance, consider a habit of smoking. A person may smoke to relieve stress, and by identifying this root cause, they can explore healthier stress management strategies. Without this understanding, any attempt to quit smoking may not be successful, as the underlying need – stress relief – would still be unaddressed.

Understanding the root cause of a habit also paves the way for habit substitution, a widely recognized method for habit change. Instead of trying to completely abolish a habit, it can be more effective to replace it with a new one. By identifying the cue and reward associated with a bad habit, a new, more beneficial behavior can be introduced to satisfy the same need. This understanding aids in designing an appropriate replacement habit that provides a similar reward.

Furthermore, comprehension of the root cause of a habit may facilitate mindfulness and self-awareness. Being cognizant of one's triggers and responses can foster proactive behavior, where one is able to intercept a potentially harmful habit before it takes hold. For example, if a person tends to eat junk food when they are bored, recognizing this pattern can help them to take action, such as engaging in a different activity when boredom strikes.

Unraveling the root cause of a habit can also contribute to a sense of self-compassion. Understanding that habits are often formed as coping mechanisms or adaptations to certain situations can reduce feelings of guilt or failure associated with the habit. This gentler perspective towards oneself can actually promote change by creating a more positive and supportive mental environment.

In essence, understanding the root cause of a habit provides a roadmap for effective habit change. It offers insight into why a habit exists, what purpose it serves, and how it can be effectively addressed. It equips individuals with the knowledge and self-awareness needed to reshape their behaviors, fostering personal growth and well-being.

How Can I Deal With Setbacks in Breaking a Bad Habit?

Embarking on the journey to break a bad habit is a commendable initiative, but one that often involves stumbling blocks and setbacks. The process is seldom linear and understanding that it's normal to face challenges along the way is crucial. Dealing with these setbacks effectively, and maintaining the motivation to persevere, hinges on the adoption of specific strategies and shifts in mindset.

Setbacks in breaking a bad habit can be reframed as opportunities for learning. Each setback can offer valuable insights into the factors that are hindering the process of breaking the habit. These could include external triggers, emotional states, or specific situations. By examining these factors, one can devise strategies to overcome them or even avoid them in the future. This active learning process can contribute significantly to eventual success in habit change.

Maintaining a solution-oriented mindset is another strategy to deal with setbacks. This involves focusing on finding ways to overcome the challenges, rather than dwelling on the setback itself. This approach keeps the focus on progress and forward movement. It's also important to remember that the ultimate goal is long-term change, and this can often take time and patience.

Developing a self-compassionate attitude can also be instrumental in dealing with setbacks. Self-compassion entails treating oneself with kindness and understanding during challenging times. Instead of berating oneself for a momentary lapse, acknowledging the difficulty of the process and forgiving oneself can help maintain morale and motivation.

Another strategy is to leverage social support. Sharing one's journey of breaking a habit with trusted friends or family members can help create a supportive environment. They can offer encouragement during setbacks and celebrate progress, which can help maintain motivation. Additionally, they might provide an outside perspective that can be useful in identifying triggers or patterns that one might not notice on their own.

Lastly, setting realistic and manageable goals can help prevent feelings of overwhelm that can lead to setbacks. It may be more effective to break down the process of habit change into smaller, more achievable steps. Celebrating these smaller victories can build confidence and motivation, making the overall task of breaking the habit seem less daunting.

Dealing with setbacks is a crucial part of the journey in breaking a bad habit. Viewing them as opportunities for learning, maintaining a solution-oriented mindset, practicing self-compassion, leveraging social support, and setting realistic goals can be effective strategies. These approaches can help navigate the challenges and keep one's momentum going towards the ultimate goal of successful habit change.

How Can I Handle Situations That Trigger My Bad Habits?

Dealing with situations that spark off undesirable habits is a critical aspect of habit change. Comprehending how triggers work and devising strategies to handle them effectively can greatly enhance the success of the process. This process often involves identification of triggers, creation of an action plan, implementation of alternative behaviors, mindfulness practice, and self-compassion.

Firstly, a clear identification of what constitutes a trigger is essential. Triggers are cues that set off the habitual behavior, and they can be anything from a certain time of day, a place, specific people, an emotional state, or a preceding action. By paying attention to the contexts in which the bad habit arises, one can become aware of these triggers, which is the first step towards managing them effectively.

Once the triggers have been identified, creating an action plan can help prepare for dealing with these situations. This could involve thinking through ways to avoid the trigger where possible. For instance, if a certain route home triggers a bad habit of stopping at a fast-food restaurant, finding an alternate route can help. If complete avoidance is not possible, the plan could involve preparing a different response to the trigger.

Implementing alternative behaviors when a trigger is encountered is another valuable strategy. Ideally, these alternatives should be satisfying in a way that's similar to the bad habit but without the negative consequences. For instance, if stress triggers a smoking habit, finding a healthier stress management technique such as exercise or deep breathing can be a viable alternative.

In addition to these active strategies, mindfulness can also be a powerful tool in handling triggers. By cultivating a state of present-moment awareness, one can learn to observe the craving that arises from the trigger without automatically reacting to it. Over time, this can weaken the power of the trigger and create space for choosing a different response.

Finally, adopting an attitude of self-compassion can be instrumental in dealing with setbacks or difficulties in managing triggers. It's normal to falter at times, especially when dealing with strong triggers. Rather than being hard on oneself, responding with kindness and understanding can help maintain the motivation to continue working on the habit change.

Handling situations that trigger bad habits involves a combination of understanding the nature of triggers, planning and executing alternative responses, practicing mindfulness, and maintaining self-compassion. This multi-faceted approach can increase the likelihood of successfully modifying bad habits and establishing healthier ones in their place.

How Can Cognitive Behavioral Therapy Help in Breaking Bad Habits?

Breaking bad habits can be an intricate process that requires not just willpower, but also a deep understanding of how these habits form, function, and can be effectively altered. One therapeutic technique that has shown substantial success in helping individuals break bad habits is cognitive behavioral therapy (CBT). Grounded in psychology, CBT combines cognitive therapy's focus on thoughts and attitudes with behavioral therapy's emphasis on actions and behavior patterns.

Central to CBT is the understanding that our thoughts, emotions, and behaviors are interconnected, implying that a change in one of these areas can lead to changes in the others. If a negative habit is viewed as a type of behavior rooted in certain thought patterns and emotional responses, it becomes clear how CBT could be instrumental in habit change. This therapy helps individuals recognize and alter negative or destructive thought patterns that lead to unwanted behaviors, substituting them with more constructive and healthier alternatives.

CBT uses various strategies to achieve these changes. For instance, cognitive restructuring, one of the main strategies used in CBT, involves identifying and challenging irrational or unhelpful thoughts. When these thoughts are associated with a bad habit, cognitive restructuring can help alter the thought patterns that support the habit. This can lead to a decrease in the frequency and intensity of the behavior.

Another critical aspect of CBT is exposure and response prevention. This technique exposes individuals to situations that trigger their bad habits and helps them resist the urge to perform the habitual behavior. Gradually, this resistance helps break the link between the trigger and the habit, facilitating the process of habit change.

Behavioral experiments are another strategy in CBT. They allow individuals to test their beliefs and assumptions about their habits in controlled situations. By observing the results, they can gain a clearer understanding of their habits, which can help them make effective changes.

Lastly, CBT often includes the use of coping strategies and problem-solving skills. These tools provide additional support for managing triggers, dealing with setbacks, and maintaining progress in breaking bad habits.

CBT provides a robust framework for understanding and altering habits. By addressing the cognitive and emotional underpinnings of habits and providing practical tools for behavior change, CBT can be an effective approach in breaking bad habits.

How Can I Be More Mindful of My Bad Habits?

The process of becoming more aware of your bad habits is fundamentally a journey of increased mindfulness. Mindfulness, the practice of paying attention in a particular way, on purpose and non-judgmentally, plays an important role in recognizing and ultimately changing our habits. By being present and truly observing our behavior, we can identify habitual patterns that we might otherwise overlook.

Your journey can start with observing your daily routines and identifying patterns of behavior that recur. For instance, do you notice a tendency to snack when you're stressed, or do you always light a cigarette when you have a cup of coffee? These behaviors can seem automatic, and you might not notice them until you deliberately start to pay attention. Mindfulness can help you catch these moments as they occur, observing them without judgment or trying to change them immediately.

After identifying these patterns, the next step is to recognize the triggers that cause these habits. Triggers could be emotional states, such as feeling anxious or bored, certain times of the day, or even specific locations. By maintaining a mindful approach, you can start to see the connection between these triggers and your habits, providing vital insights into why and when these behaviors occur.

You can then begin to observe the consequences of your habits. How do you feel after engaging in the behavior? Is there a sense of relief, guilt, or discomfort? Recognizing the immediate and long-term effects of your habits can help you understand the reward your brain is seeking, an essential component of the habit loop. This understanding can motivate you to change the behavior and seek healthier rewards.

A useful tool for developing mindfulness is meditation. Regular practice can enhance your ability to stay present and focused, which is crucial for habit awareness. Even just a few minutes each day can help increase your mindfulness and make you more aware of your habits.

Another technique is to journal about your habits. Writing about your habits, their triggers, and consequences can help solidify your observations and make you more consciously aware of your patterns. It also provides a tangible record that you can refer back to, tracking your progress over time.

Being more mindful of your bad habits involves a commitment to observing and understanding your behavior in a non-judgmental way. By identifying patterns, recognizing triggers and consequences, and using tools like meditation and journaling, you can become more aware of your habits and take the first steps toward change.

How Can A Habit Bridge Help Me To Break A Bad Habit?

Creating a "bridge habit" is an innovative approach in the field of habit change. This concept hinges on the notion of creating an intermediary habit that closely resembles the old habit in its form but varies greatly in terms of content and potential harm. A bridge habit is essentially a 'place-holder' that reduces the shock of sudden change, making the transition smoother. It allows individuals to feel the comfort of a familiar routine while gradually distancing themselves from the harmful aspects of the bad habit.

For instance, consider the case of Richard, a heavy scotch drinker. Like many individuals striving to break a detrimental habit, Richard faced the daunting task of not only eradicating the physical act of drinking scotch but also dealing with the ingrained routine associated with it. The bridge habit he devised ingeniously tackled both these aspects.

By replacing the scotch in the bottle with tea, Richard found a healthier substitute for the harmful substance itself. Yet, he didn't stop there. He poured the tea into the same type of bottle and even used the same rocks glass to drink it, thereby maintaining the routine and the rituals he associated with the habit. The bottle still looked like a bottle of scotch, and the process of pouring and drinking remained unchanged, thus preserving the comfort and familiarity of the old routine.

Let's consider another creative example. Suppose Lisa has a habit of scrolling through social media for hours before bed, affecting her sleep quality. To change this, she could implement a bridge habit. Instead of trying to quit cold turkey, she could switch her late-night scrolling from social media to an e-book reader app with a dark mode and no notifications. She'd still be scrolling on her device, which feels familiar, but the content would be more focused and less stimulating, reducing the chances of disrupted sleep.

In both these scenarios, the bridge habit serves as a stepping stone, a bridge that helps individuals traverse the chasm between their old, damaging habits and their new, healthier ones. It's a clever method that leverages the power of familiarity and routine while transforming the core of the habit, making habit change more achievable and less daunting.

Consider Sandra, who has a habit of reaching for sugary snacks when she's stressed. She could introduce a bridge habit, such as swapping out candy bars for pieces of fresh fruit or a handful of dried fruits and nuts. They're both snacks she can grab when stressed, but one is healthier and can fulfill the same need for a quick energy boost and stress relief.

Now, let's imagine the case of Alex, who spends a significant amount of time playing video games, leading to sedentary behavior. Instead of trying to stop playing games altogether, he could shift his interest towards active gaming or exergames that require physical movement to play. Here, the thrill of gaming remains constant, but the sedentary nature of the activity changes.

Then there's Maria, a workaholic who rarely takes breaks, leading to burnout. As a bridge habit, Maria can start by taking 'working breaks.' During these breaks, she could read industry-related articles or attend online seminars. This way, she still feels productive (thus satisfying her workaholic tendencies), but she's also giving herself a break from her regular work tasks.

Finally, take the case of Tom, who has the habit of smoking when he takes breaks at work. A potential bridge habit could be to keep a stress ball or a fidget spinner at his desk. Each time he feels the urge to smoke, he instead uses these tools to keep his hands busy and divert his mind, keeping the 'break' aspect of his habit while removing the harmful element.

These examples illustrate the potential of bridge habits. They allow people to maintain a sense of routine and familiarity, making the process of changing habits less intimidating and more manageable. Remember, the key to a successful bridge habit is to ensure it meets the same needs as the old habit but in a healthier or more productive way.

Keep in mind that a habit bridge may be transformed from an intermediary habit to a completely new and permanent habit. In Sandra's case, the fruits and nuts she substituted for sugary snacks can become a new habit. In Richard's case, he may decide to no longer mimic his past alcohol consumption with ice tea in a liquor bottle. Richard may simply decide unlink his current enjoyment of tea from his past enjoyment of alcohol and simply drink his tea from a standard water glass.

67

Conclusion

In the chapters that preceded this, we embarked on an enlightening journey, dissecting the intricate world of habits – the good, the bad, and the ugly. We discovered how habits are formed, how they are maintained, and most importantly, how they can be changed. We delved into topics as diverse as willpower, stress, cognitive behavioral therapy, mindfulness, and the role they all play in habit formation and alteration. We unraveled the complex relationship between our daily routines and the underlying psychological processes that fuel them.

Our exploration revealed that, contrary to popular belief, it is not always about eliminating a habit, but rather replacing it with a healthier one. We discussed the concept of 'bridge habits', illustrating how these intermediary habits can act as stepping stones towards the final goal of habit change. They create a smoother transition and offer an effective strategy to deal with cravings and avoid falling back into old habits.

We highlighted the importance of understanding the root cause of a habit, as it plays a pivotal role in breaking it. We also shed light on how setbacks are part and parcel of the habit change process, and how they should not deter us from our ultimate goals. Stress, we learned, can be a significant roadblock in our journey towards breaking bad habits, emphasizing the need for stress management strategies.

We discovered how mindfulness and cognitive behavioral therapy can be beneficial in recognizing and altering habits. These techniques equip us with the skills to be aware of our actions, understand the triggers and consequences, and strategically plan our responses.

In summary, breaking bad habits is not a sprint, but a marathon. It requires a deep understanding of oneself, patience, resilience, and the right techniques. It's a journey of self-discovery and growth. So, here's to embracing the challenge of change, to learning and growing, and to becoming the best versions of ourselves.

This book was written in the hope that it would serve as a guide to help you navigate your own journey of breaking bad habits. It's a small step towards creating a better, healthier, and more fulfilling life. If there's one thing to take away from this book, let it be this: change is possible, and you have the power to make it happen.

Stay curious, stay resilient, and remember - every day is a new opportunity for transformation..

A Personal Thank You

To every reader who chose to embark on this journey of understanding and transformation, I extend my deepest gratitude. You made the choice to delve into the depths of your habits, to confront, understand, and alter them. The commitment, curiosity, and courage that involves is something I profoundly admire.

Your willingness to explore these pages is a testament to your dedication to growth and learning. That you've sought to better understand the intricacies of your own behaviors and habits, and, in doing so, improve your own life and potentially the lives of those around you, is inspiring.

Thank you for entrusting me with your time and attention. Writing this book has been an enlightening journey, filled with discoveries, challenges, and immense personal growth. Your engagement with this work has made that journey worthwhile.

My hope is that the knowledge and strategies shared in these pages will serve as valuable tools in your own journey of personal transformation. May they guide you towards healthier, more fulfilling habits, and ultimately towards a richer and more rewarding life.

Once again, from the bottom of my heart, thank you. I wish you all the success in your future endeavors and remember, the power to change lies within you.

With Deepest Gratitude,

Tyson Phanann

Visit Our Website for More Personal Development Information

The journey of understanding and reshaping habits is a continuous one, filled with both triumphs and challenges. It's a journey that can lead to remarkable transformations, improved well-being, and a deeper understanding of oneself. While this book has been designed to provide a comprehensive look into habits and strategies for change, there's always more to explore.

Therefore, I cordially invite you to visit my website, **AchieveProgress.com**. Here, you'll find a wealth of additional resources and material to help you on your journey. OurWebsite.com is a platform designed for those who want to delve deeper, offering articles, videos, interactive tools, and a vibrant community dedicated to personal growth and transformation.

On **AchieveProgress.com**, you can expect regular updates on cutting-edge research, insightful blog posts from a range of experts, practical tools for habit change, and inspirational success stories from people just like you. Moreover, it's a place for dialogue - an opportunity to share your experiences, ask questions, and gain support from a community who, like you, are committed to their own personal development journey.

This book is just the beginning. Allow **AchieveProgress.com** to be your guide, your community, and your source of ongoing inspiration and knowledge as you continue your journey towards mastering your habits.

Thank you for your interest and commitment to self-improvement. I look forward to connecting with you on **AchieveProgress.com** and hearing about your journey.

See you there!

AchieveProgress.com

Notes

What Is A Habit?

Clear, J. (2018). Atomic Habits: An Easy & Proven Way to Build Good Habits & Break Bad Ones. Penguin Random House.

Duhigg, C. (2014). The Power of Habit: Why We Do What We Do in Life and Business. Random House Trade Paperbacks.

Lally, P., & Gardner, B. (2013). Promoting habit formation. Health Psychology Review, 7(sup1), S137-S158.

Eyal, N., & Hoover, R. (2014). Hooked: How to Build Habit-Forming Products. Portfolio/Penguin.

How Do I Create a New Habit?

Clear, J. (2018). Atomic Habits: An Easy & Proven Way to Build Good Habits & Break Bad Ones. Penguin Random House.

Duhigg, C. (2014). The Power of Habit: Why We Do What We Do in Life and Business. Random House Trade Paperbacks.

Neal, D. T., Wood, W., & Quinn, J. M. (2006). Habits—A repeat performance. Current Directions in Psychological Science, 15(4), 198-202.

Ouellette, J. A., & Wood, W. (1998). Habit and intention in everyday life: The multiple processes by which past behavior predicts future behavior. Psychological Bulletin, 124(1), 54-74.

What Are the Best Strategies to Form Good Habits?

Clear, J. (2018). Atomic Habits: An Easy & Proven Way to Build Good Habits & Break Bad Ones. Penguin Random House.

Duhigg, C. (2014). The Power of Habit: Why We Do What We Do in Life and Business. Random House Trade Paperbacks.

Schunk, D. H. (2012). Learning Theories: An Educational Perspective (6th Edition). Pearson.

Lally, P., van Jaarsveld, C. H. M., Potts, H. W. W., & Wardle, J. (2010). How are habits formed: Modelling habit formation in the real world. European Journal of Social Psychology, 40(6), 998-1009.

How Long Does It Take to Form a New Habit?

Lally, P., van Jaarsveld, C. H. M., Potts, H. W. W., & Wardle, J. (2010). How are habits formed: Modelling habit formation in the real world. European Journal of Social Psychology, 40(6), 998-1009.

Maltz, M. (1960). Psycho-Cybernetics: A New Technique for Using Your Subconscious Power. Prentice-Hall.

Kleim, J. A., & Jones, T. A. (2008). Principles of experience-dependent neural plasticity: implications for rehabilitation after brain damage. Journal of Speech, Language, and Hearing Research, 51(1), S225-S239.

Clear, J. (2018). Atomic

How Can I Make My Habits Stick?

Clear, J. (2018). Atomic Habits: An Easy & Proven Way to Build Good Habits & Break Bad Ones. Penguin Random House.

Duhigg, C. (2014). The Power of Habit: Why We Do What We Do in Life and Business. Random House Trade Paperbacks.

Hebb, D. O. (1949). The Organization of Behavior: A Neuropsychological Theory. Wiley & Sons.

Lally, P., van Jaarsveld, C. H. M., Potts, H. W. W., & Wardle, J. (2010). How are habits formed: Modelling habit formation in the real world. European Journal of Social Psychology, 40(6), 998-1009.

How Can I Make My Habits Automatic?

Clear, J. (2018). Atomic Habits: An Easy & Proven Way to Build Good Habits & Break Bad Ones. Penguin Random House.

Duhigg, C. (2014). The Power of Habit: Why We Do What We Do in Life and Business. Random House Trade Paperbacks.

Lally, P., van Jaarsveld, C. H. M., Potts, H. W. W., & Wardle, J. (2010). How are habits formed: Modelling habit formation in the real world. European Journal of Social Psychology, 40(6), 998-1009.

Imamura, K. (2012). Kaizen: The key to Japan's competitive success. McGraw-Hill/Irwin.

What Role Does Motivation Play in Forming Good Habits?

Bandura, A. (1977). Self-efficacy: Toward a Unifying Theory of Behavioral Change. Psychological Review, 84(2), 191-215.

Clear, J. (2018). Atomic Habits: An Easy & Proven Way to Build Good Habits & Break Bad Ones. Penguin Random House.

Duhigg, C. (2014). The Power of Habit: Why We Do What We Do in Life and Business. Random House Trade Paperbacks.

Locke, E. A., & Latham, G. P. (2006). New directions in goal-setting theory. Current Directions in Psychological Science, 15(5), 265-268.

How Can I Keep Track of My Habits?

Clear, J. (2018). Atomic Habits: An Easy & Proven Way to Build Good Habits & Break Bad Ones. Penguin Random House.

Duhigg, C. (2014). The Power of Habit: Why We Do What We Do in Life and Business. Random House Trade Paperbacks.

Fogg, B. J. (2019). Tiny Habits: The Small Changes That Change Everything. Houghton Mifflin Harcourt.

What Are Some Good Habits That Can Improve My Life?

World Health Organization. (2020). Physical activity.

National Sleep Foundation. (2015). How Much Sleep Do We Really Need?

Harvard Health Publishing. (2021). Mindful eating. Harvard University.

American Psychological Association. (2012). Benefits of Lifelong Learning.

Emmons, R. A., & McCullough, M. E. (2003). Counting blessings versus burdens: An experimental investigation of gratitude and subjective well-being in daily life. Journal of Personality and Social Psychology.

Can A Good Habit Replace A Bad One?

Clear, J. (2018). Atomic Habits: An Easy & Proven Way to Build Good Habits & Break Bad Ones. Avery.

Wood, W., & Neal, D. T. (2007). A new look at habits and the habit-goal interface. Psychological Review.

Lally, P., van Jaarsveld, C. H., Potts, H. W., & Wardle, J. (2010). How are habits formed: Modelling habit formation in the real world. European Journal of Social Psychology.

How Can I Be Consistent in My Habits?

Clear, J. (2018). Atomic Habits: An Easy & Proven Way to Build Good Habits & Break Bad Ones. Avery.

Gollwitzer, P. M. (1999). Implementation intentions: Strong effects of simple plans. American Psychologist.

How Does Habit Stacking Work?

Clear, J. (2018). Atomic Habits: An Easy & Proven Way to Build Good Habits & Break Bad Ones. Avery.

Duhigg, C. (2012). The Power of Habit: Why We Do What We Do in Life and Business. Random House.

How Important is the Environment in Habit Formation?

Wood, W., & Neal, D. T. (2007). A new look at habits and the habit-goal interface. Psychological review, 114(4), 843.

Neal, D. T., Wood, W., Labrecque, J. S., & Lally, P. (2012). How do habits guide behavior? Perceived and actual triggers of habits in daily life. Journal of Experimental Social Psychology, 48(2), 492-498.

Christakis, N. A., & Fowler, J. H. (2007). The spread of obesity in a large social network over 32 years. New England journal of medicine, 357(4), 370-379.

How Can I Use Triggers or Cues to Form Good Habits?

Duhigg, C. (2012). The Power of Habit: Why We Do What We Do in Life and Business. Random House.

Wood, W., & Neal, D. T. (2007). A new look at habits and the habit-goal interface. Psychological review, 114(4), 843.

Lally, P., Van Jaarsveld, C. H., Potts, H. W., & Wardle, J. (2010). How are habits formed: Modelling habit formation in the real world. European Journal of Social Psychology, 40(6), 998-1009.

How Can Habits Improve My Productivity?

Clear, J. (2018). Atomic Habits: An Easy & Proven Way to Build Good Habits & Break Bad Ones. Avery.

Baumeister, R. F., & Tierney, J. (2012). Willpower: Rediscovering the Greatest Human Strength. Penguin Press.

Duhigg, C. (2012). The Power of Habit: Why We Do What We Do in Life and Business. Random House.

How Do I Set Realistic Goals for My Habits?

Clear, J. (2018). Atomic Habits: An Easy & Proven Way to Build Good Habits & Break Bad Ones. Avery.

Doran, G. T. (1981). There's a S.M.A.R.T. way to write management's goals and objectives. Management Review, Volume 70, Issue 11(AMA FORUM), pp. 35-36.

Locke, E. A., & Latham, G. P. (2006). New directions in goal-setting theory. Current Directions in Psychological Science, 15(5), 265-268.

How Do I Break a Bad Habit?

Duhigg, C. (2012). The Power of Habit: Why We Do What We Do in Life and Business. Random House.

Neal, D. T., Wood, W., & Quinn, J. M. (2006). Habits—A Repeat Performance. Current Directions in Psychological Science, 15(4), 198–202.

What are the Best Strategies to Break Bad Habits?

Duhigg, C. (2012). The Power of Habit: Why We Do What We Do in Life and Business. Random House.

Imai, M. (1986). Kaizen: The key to Japan's competitive success. New York: Random House Business Division.

Wood, W., & Neal, D. T. (2007). A new look at habits and the habit-goal interface. Psychological Review, 114(4), 843–863.

How Long Does it Take to Break a Habit?

Lally, P., Van Jaarsveld, C. H. M., Potts, H. W. W., & Wardle, J. (2010). How are habits formed: Modelling habit formation in the real world. European Journal of Social Psychology, 40(6), 998–1009.

Maltz, M. (1960). Psycho-Cybernetics. Simon & Schuster.

How Can I Replace a Bad Habit with a Good One?

Duhigg, C. (2012). The Power of Habit: Why We Do What We Do in Life and Business. Random House.

How Can I Deal with the Cravings that Come When Trying to Break a Habit?

Ong, J. C., Ulmer, C. S., & Manber, R. (2012). Improving sleep with mindfulness and acceptance: a metacognitive model of insomnia. Behaviour research and therapy, 50(11), 651-660.

Tang, Y. Y., Tang, R., & Posner, M. I. (2016). Mindfulness meditation improves emotion regulation and reduces drug abuse. Drug and alcohol dependence, 163, S13-S18.

Can I Completely Eliminate a Habit, or Does it Just Get Replaced?

Hebb, D. O. (1949). The Organization of Behavior. New York: Wiley & Sons.

Duhigg, Charles. (2012). The Power of Habit: Why We Do What We Do in Life and Business. Random House.

Schwarts, J., & Gladding, R. (2011). You Are Not Your Brain: The 4-Step Solution for Changing Bad Habits, Ending Unhealthy Thinking, and Taking Control of Your Life. Avery Publishing.

How Can I Keep Myself Motivated While Trying to Break a Bad Habit?

Locke, E. A., & Latham, G. P. (2002). Building a practically useful theory of goal setting and task motivation. American Psychologist, 57(9), 705-717.

Neff, K. D. (2003). The development and validation of a scale to measure self-compassion. Self and Identity, 2(3), 223-250.

Kabat-Zinn, J. (2003). Mindfulness-Based

What Role Does Willpower Play in Breaking Bad Habits?

Baumeister, R. F., & Tierney, J. (2011). Willpower: Rediscovering the Greatest Human Strength. New York: Penguin Press.

Job, V., Dweck, C. S., & Walton, G. M. (2010). Ego Depletion—Is It All in Your Head?: Implicit Theories About Willpower Affect Self-Regulation. Psychological Science, 21(11), 1686-1693.

Wood, W., & Neal, D. T. (2007). A New Look at Habits and the Habit-Goal Interface. Psychological Review, 114(4), 843-863.

How Does Stress Affect Bad Habits?

Sinha, R. (2008). Chronic stress, drug use, and vulnerability to addiction. Annals of the New York Academy of Sciences, 1141, 105-130.

Schwabe, L., & Wolf, O. T. (2011). Stress-induced modulation of instrumental behavior: From goal-directed to habitual control of action. Behavioural Brain Research, 219(2), 321-328.

Shiffman, S., Paty, J. A., Gnys, M., Kassel, J. A., & Elash, C. (1995). Nicotine withdrawal in chippers and regular smokers: Subjective and cognitive effects. Health Psychology, 14(4), 301–309.

How Can I Avoid Falling Back Into Old Habits?

Duhigg, C. (2012). The Power of Habit: Why We Do What We Do in Life and Business. Random House.

Neal, D. T., Wood, W., & Quinn, J. M. (2006). Habits—A Repeat Performance. Current Directions in Psychological Science, 15(4), 198-202.

Lally, P., Van Jaarsveld, C. H. M., Potts, H. W. W., & Wardle, J. (2010). How are habits formed: Modelling habit formation in the real world. European Journal of Social Psychology, 40(6), 998-1009.

How Does Understanding the Root Cause of a Habit Help in Breaking It?

Duhigg, C. (2012). The Power of Habit: Why We Do What We Do in Life and Business. Random House.

Neal, D. T., Wood, W., & Quinn, J. M. (2006). Habits—A Repeat Performance. Current Directions in Psychological Science, 15(4), 198-202.

Lally, P., Van Jaarsveld, C. H. M., Potts, H. W. W., & Wardle, J. (2010). How are habits formed: Modelling habit formation in the real world. European Journal of Social Psychology, 40(6), 998-1009.

Neff, K. D., & Germer, C. K. (2013). A pilot study and randomized controlled trial of the mindful self-compassion program. Journal of Clinical Psychology, 69(1), 28-44.

How Can I Deal With the Setbacks in Breaking a Bad Habit?

Neff, K. D., & Germer, C. K. (2013). A pilot study and randomized controlled trial of the mindful self-compassion program. Journal of Clinical Psychology, 69(1), 28-44.

Locke, E. A., & Latham, G. P. (2002). Building a practically useful theory of goal setting and task motivation: A 35-year odyssey. American Psychologist, 57(9), 705-717.

Duhigg, C. (2012). The Power of Habit: Why We Do What We Do in Life and Business. Random House.

Lally, P., Van Jaarsveld, C. H. M., Potts, H. W. W., & Wardle, J. (2010). How are habits formed: Modelling habit formation in the real world. European Journal of Social Psychology, 40(6), 998-1009.

Kelly, J. F., & White, W. L. (2012). Broadening the Base of Addiction Mutual-Help Organizations. Journal of Groups in Addiction & Recovery, 7(2-4), 82-101.

How Can I Handle Situations That Trigger My Bad Habits?

Oaten, M., & Cheng, K. (2006). Improved self-control: The benefits of a regular program of academic study. Basic and Applied Social Psychology, 28(1), 1-16.

Kabat-Zinn, J. (2003). Mindfulness-Based Interventions in Context: Past, Present, and Future. Clinical Psychology: Science and Practice, 10(2), 144-156.

Neff, K. (2011). Self-Compassion, Self-esteem, and Well-being. Social and Personality Psychology Compass, 5(1), 1-12.

Duhigg, C. (2012). The Power of Habit: Why We Do What We Do in Life and Business. Random House.

Skinner, B. F. (1953). Science and human behavior. Simon and Schuster.

How Can Cognitive Behavioral Therapy Help in Breaking Bad Habits?

Beck, J. S. (2011). Cognitive behavior therapy: Basics and beyond. Guilford Press.

O'Connor, K. P., Aardema, F., & Pelissier, M. C. (2005). Beyond Reasonable Doubt: Reasoning Processes in Obsessive-Compulsive Disorder and Related Disorders. Wiley.

Leahy, R. L., & Holland, S. J. (2000). Treatment plans and interventions for depression and anxiety disorders. Guilford Press.

Hofmann, S. G., Asnaani, A., Vonk, I. J., Sawyer, A. T., & Fang, A. (2012). The Efficacy of Cognitive Behavioral Therapy: A Review of Meta-analyses. Cognitive Therapy and Research, 36(5), 427-440.

How Can I Be More Mindful of My Bad Habits?

Kabat-Zinn, J. (2009). Wherever you go, there you are: Mindfulness meditation in everyday life. Hachette UK.

Albers, S. (2008). Eating mindfully: How to end mindless eating and enjoy a balanced relationship with food. New Harbinger Publications.

Brewer, J. (2019). The Craving Mind: From Cigarettes to Smartphones to Love—Why We Get Hooked and How We Can Break Bad Habits. Yale University Press.

Chiesa, A., & Serretti, A. (2010). A systematic review of neurobiological and clinical features of mindfulness meditations. Psychological Medicine, 40(8), 1239-1252.

Copyright and Disclaimer

www.ingramcontent.com/pod-product-compliance
Lightning Source LLC
Chambersburg PA
CBHW070547160726
48003CB00005B/1926